Beautiful America's
Oregon

Cover - Mt. Hood / Craig Tuttle

Revised Edition © 1995
Published by
Beautiful America Publishing Co.
9725 S.W. Commerce Circle
Wilsonville, Oregon 97070

Library of Congress Cataloging in Publication Data
Beautiful America's Oregon
1. Oregon — Description and Travel — 1981— Views.
I. Beautiful America (Firm)   II. Title   III. Title: Oregon
F877.C86   1987   917.95   87-19565
ISBN 0-89802-432-3
ISBN 0-89802-428-5 (Paperback)

Willamette Valley Wine Grapes / Craig Tuttle

Beautiful America's
Oregon

Text by Gail M. Curtis

For my mom.

Contents

Behold The Beauty Of Oregon

A friend once told me that there is a definite order to things in life. When you look at the overall scheme, he said, you'll see that we can't all be master composers capable of touching hearts with every piece of music we write. There is a place for Mozart and a place for Salieri, and no matter how earnestly one struggles to get the word out about the treasures inherent in a particular artist's work, some people will always be famous; others will remain relatively unknown. The great thing about accepting that premise is discovering that unique pleasure can be derived from each.

The same premise holds true for Oregon. Here, there are majestic wonders, unparalleled in many parts of the country, from the monumental beauty of the snow-covered Cascades to the dashing excitement of the rugged Oregon beaches. Visitors find an abundance of sights well-known through the glossy postcards of family and friends, or the travel section of their local newspapers. They find landmarks visible by plaques describing their historical or geological significance. They find deserving spots—like Multnomah Falls, Crater Lake, and southern Oregon beaches—which prompt the much sought-after ooooohs and aaaaahs.

But the great thing about Oregon is that here we have the wonder of lesser known pleasures, too. These may be microscopic beauties in the scheme of things, familiar only to the few who venture off the beaten path (and would just as soon keep it that way), but they are treasures just the same. They are the gentle surprise of a miniature waterfall trickling down a moss-covered ledge, or the sudden impact of a brilliant stone polished by a rush of mountain water. They are experiences of the moment like finding an arrowhead in a dusty field, perhaps not phenomenal in itself, but also not meant to be missed. The beauty of Oregon is found in

Portland's Pittock Mansion / Craig Tuttle

(Opposite) Riverplace Marina and Portland Skyline / Craig Tuttle

every corner, in every crevice, and at every level of that great order. It's the challenge of the individual to put it all into perspective.

Which brings us back to the familiar—beauty is in the eyes of the beholder. It's still true, but in Oregon, the search extends a few senses further. Here, it is found in the eyes, ears, nose, throat and fingers of the beholder. It's simply impossible to take a tiny peek at Mt. Hood, or a little whiff of Seaside air. One can't listen just a bit to a cascading waterfall or lightly touch and taste a plump strawberry. Oregon is a state to be grasped. It is a place for visitors and residents to feast the senses, and wallow in the many joys that the Oregon wilderness and communities have to offer.

As a past midwesterner and present Oregonian (known locally as "transplant"), I know outsiders have preconceived notions of this place, and residents do, too. And when you stop to think about it, what really is a state, but a compilation of perceptions, both individual and group, past and present, distorted and true? Oregon gets its image in the same way as the other 49. So how does one sift through all those viewpoints and grasp the true flavor? Just what is it about Oregon that makes it unique? As you stroll through the pages in this book, you'll discover for yourself. I'll keep the journey simple by keying on visions of the state from an outside perspective, and taking a closer look at those notions from an inside perspective. The final perspective is up to you.

Look at the photographs in this book, not only for the scenic beauty they capture, but for the geographic and climatic variations of the state. Here, we have a small valley so laden with sand dunes, it conjures up images of camel caravans. We also have high desert country which is dry and barren in the summer, and snow-covered in the winter. We have a rocky coastline edged by the cool Pacific, and an internal boundary, in the form of the Cascade Range, which includes a string of presently dormant volcanoes. The largest river of the West provides us with an unusual, near sea-level passageway through mountains and desert. In the western part of the state, we have fertile river valleys abundant with produce. And we didn't get that image of flannel-shirted lumberjacks for nothing, because we're also the place with all those conifers reaching upward toward all that rain. Which brings us to perhaps the most frequently asked question—the big one. Just how much does it rain here anyway? You'll find out later.

Oregon communities are as diverse as the geography of the lands they're found in, which is apparent by the names of our towns. We have a town touted by locals as "Bandon-by-the-Sea," another whose Latin name, Corvallis, means "heart of the valley." We even have a relic of a town in northeast Oregon called Fossil. There's a Madras, a Philomath, a John Day, and maybe because we're not as unique as we think we are, we also have a St. Paul, a Detroit, and a Dallas. If it weren't for the luck of an early settler from Portland, Maine, who won the right through a toss of a coin to give a name to that settlement off the Columbia, just upstream on the Willamette—now called Portland—we would also have a Boston.

And yes, there is culture, in this wild wilderness of a state. While we do have bucking bronco action at the Pendleton Round-Up, we also have fancy footwork at the performing arts centers in Portland and Eugene. For aficionados of sculpture, there are the wave-carved rocks along the southern coast, as well as man-carved ones in the Oregon Art Institute. And where else but in Oregon, could a person savor a soliloquy and a log rolling contest on the very same weekend? Oregon satisfies a wide range of tastes, from a passion for Moe's clam chowder, to farm fresh filberts, and yes, I do mean soup to nuts.

Washington Park's Japanese Gardens / Craig Tuttle

The Sternwheeler - Columbia Gorge / Kenneth Naversen

Oregon is for the active of heart, body and soul. People here fish for trout in mountain streams or dig for clams on coastal beaches. While the state has been called a runner's mecca, it could also rightly be called a biker's haven, and a kayaker's paradise. Thanks to Mt. Hood, it's the only place in the lower 48 where you can ski all year round. And thanks to ideal winds in the mid Columbia Gorge, there's a spot that's earned the title "Windsurfing capital of the world." In Oregon, the adventurous can take a llama trek into the Wallowa Mountains. And the curious can explore endless miles of backroads, complete with covered bridges, old-time auctions, and real-live ghost towns.

In a whirlwind overview of the state, Washington Park Zoo breeds more Asian elephants than anywhere outside of Asia. The Pacific Flyway in southern Oregon has the largest wintering population of bald eagles in the contiguous United States. Western Oregon has Oregon City, the first town to be incorporated west of the Mississippi. Eastern Oregon has Huntington, a town that wants to secede from its county. And Portland has the only advertising museum in the world (or so they claim), right in Old Town. At risk of sounding superfluous, many Oregonians feel that you can find just about anything you're looking for, including a great lifestyle and a clean environment, right here in this patch of land bordered by Nevada, California, the Pacific Ocean, Washington, and Idaho.

Through the double-barreled vision of a transplant who has viewed the state both from the plains 2,000 miles away, as well as right outside my back door, Oregon is nothing if not a land of diversity. We slid right into a slot waiting to be filled in the great scheme of things. In Oregon, we have a time and a place for everything.

O.K. Meriwether,
Paddle Your Own Canoe

You've probably heard the story. Meriwether Lewis and William Clark were paddling down the scenic Columbia River, when Lewis took time out to make a few leisurely notes in his well-worn journal. Clark, weary from a particularly exhausting day at the helm, suggested that if ole Meriwether had time to spare before they reached the big, blue Pacific, perhaps he should paddle his own canoe. Lewis opted to get on with the journey.

O.K., maybe it didn't really happen, but the point is it could have. After all, the now-legendary explorers were human, and what's more, the scenery of the Columbia Gorge is so unmatched in its natural beauty that it's not surprising that any writer would need time out from the mainstream of life to adequately record his observations.

The Columbia Gorge is simply majestic. Miles of scenery stand for the most part untouched, from acres of forested hillsides to undulating blanket-like hills covered with fuzzy vegetation, all in contrast to the clear, deep blue of the water. It's an area steeped in history, thanks to the detailed journals of that early pair, and the many noble adventurers who followed. With a squint of the eyes, today's traveler in the windwhipped gorge can almost feel a part of that history. There's a kind of quiet reverence about the place, perhaps in respect for the dauntless spirit of the team who blazed the way for future Oregonians.

The Columbia was actually the last leg of the journey west. Our forefathers traveled by land on the Oregon Trail until they reached what Lewis and Clark called "the trough," which, translated, means "The Dalles." There, some opted against risking life and limb to continue the journey by

The State Capitol, Salem / Zane Holland

Willamette Valley Vineyard / Craig Tuttle

water, and settled at what was then Fort Dalles. Today, historical buildings at the site of the fort stand as testimony for what was the end of the Oregon Trail to many.

Farther downstream, present day travelers can take in the sensual wonders of the mid-Columbia part of the gorge. The climate and topography in this region of Oregon has been compared to the romantic Rhine River area of Germany. Such similarity explains the abundant apple and pear orchards, and wineries, which offer excellent samples of vinifera and fruit wines.

Appropriately set in this rich river-bank countryside is an Oregon style castle—the Columbia Gorge Hotel. Built in 1921, this classic inn captures the flavor of the Roaring 20's and the soul of the many jazz musicians who were frequent guests there over six decades ago.

Our forefathers who continued downstream soon reached the "Cascades of the Columbia," a rapids at what is now Cascade Locks. This challenging section of the river forced adventurers to portage in order to continue their journey, a feat that is re-enacted every August by the community of Cascade Locks in their town's Portage Days celebration. These rapids also provided the inspiration for colorful Indian legends. Story has it that a natural stone bridge spanned the river where today's "Bridge of the Gods" connects Cascade Locks with Washington. The Great Spirit, irritated with the "warring" mountains in the Cascade chain—Wyeast (Mt. Hood) and Klickitat (Washington's Mt. Adams)—demolished the bridge, leaving it in treacherous pieces in the water below. Lo-wit, better known as Mt. St. Helens, and the only one still "warring" today, was the guardian of the bridge. Perhaps her recurring hot ash and smoke plumes are evidence that she's still a mite miffed.

In the lower gorge, Sunday drivers (or Monday through Saturday, for that matter) can travel on a section of the first highway that made the

Tulip Farm near Monitor / Craig Tuttle

gorge accessible to modern transportation. Built from 1913 to 1915, Columbia River Scenic Highway (Old U.S. 30) is now regarded as a historic engineering accomplishment. It's difficult to imagine early surveyors with primitive measuring devices responsible for a road of such longevity. The highway is still in use today in two segments—a 24 mile stretch east from Troutdale, and a 15 mile portion between Hood River and The Dalles.

Near Corbett, Vista House stands on the crest of a hillside, offering an often windy, but breathtaking view that extends for 30 miles in three directions. The house, which opened in 1918, was built as a memorial to Oregon's pioneers.

Farther downstream is the Lewis and Clark State Park, which features a hiking trail lined with the grasses, shrubs and wildflowers the explorers described in their journals.

And farther yet is the strategic location just off the Columbia, slightly upstream on the Willamette, now known as Portland. From early days, the city was one of the Pacific Northwest's chief export centers, a recognition which blossomed from the California gold rush days, through the steamboat era, to present day commerce. Today's travelers can step back in time in Old Town section of Portland, now a National Historic Landmark District. Walking tours through the area highlight early architecture of the city, much of which has been recently renovated or preserved. Museums, antique and specialty shops, as well as the Skidmore Fountain which was the popular hang-out at the turn of the century, add to the color of an earlier time.

West of Portland is Sauvie Island, another landing point for Lewis and Clark. The largest inland island in the United Sates, Sauvie Island was once called Wapato Island after the abundant beds of the vegetable "wappato" (Indian for a cross between an onion and a potato) growing there. Today, the fertile island is a major wintering spot for ducks, geese, swans, sandhill cranes and many species of small birds. Its beaches and country roads are also popular summer getaways for Portlanders.

The settlers who continued west formed the logging communities of Columbia City and St. Helens in the mid 1800's. Although the entire western portion of the river was always viewed as a vital commercial link, it also presented a major obstacle to 19th century fur traders and pioneers. Even today, barge traffic moves slowly through the gorge, proof of the risks that early travelers faced in navigating the Columbia before the construction of dams and navigational locks.

The Columbia River is a geological rarity in that it cuts a swath through hilly, rocky, mountainous and desert terrain, all the while remaining near sea level. It was long ago that the natural canal earned its place in that hierarchy of American waterways as the "Great River of the West." Today, from a historical, scenic, conservational and commercial perspective, the title is still apt.

Meriwether would be proud.

Slugs. You Learn To Love 'Em.

The slant is a sly one, probably started by jealous journalists working for boring newspapers in ugly cities throughout the United States. These envious pens paint a depressingly soggy picture of Oregon.

Because of the wet climate, they say, Oregon has slugs, so big and abundant, the prepared hiker brings a special knife just to scrape them off his boots. There are so many, they sneer, Oregon artists engage them to

Whitewater Rafting on the McKenzie River / Kenneth Naversen

(Opposite) Keene Creek in the Siskiyous / Lynn Radeka

slither across canvasses, leaving trails of landscape paintings behind. And if it weren't for Lewis and Clark, they simper, (you know, those guys who fended off an army of the slinky critters before slipping—literally—into the Columbia River) the state of Oregon would be entirely slimed over.

Well, it's just not true. There is a sliver of truth to that slander about slug paintings. But the real story is that they were abstract paintings, and the little squirms were from Washington state.

The unharsh reality is that there are some slugs here, but only in the western part of the state. They are harmless little creatures which come in delicate shades of green and brown, have slender backs, teeny little antennae, and are really kind of pretty, especially when spotted under damp leaves next to moss-covered tree trunks, in places so still and untouched, there's a kind of hush (or is that sqush) all over the world tonight, if you know what I mean. I'd simply like to say that slugs, while increasing in popularity back east, have always been vogue in Oregon. (So, outsiders, eat your hearts out and let's get on with the story.)

Because of the widespread propaganda about our weather, there are a couple points I'd like to clear up. First of all, it does rain in Oregon; secondly, not all the time. While we do have some precipitation in every corner of the state, we also have several different climates with at least four definite seasons in each, and one area of the state that even claims to have five. These seasons bring us all the standard elements of weather that you'd expect to find anywhere: rain, hail, sleet, snow, a variety of cloud forms, wind, and sun. But, to dispel any stubborn, remaining myths about Oregon weather, let's concentrate for a while on the sun.

Take southern Oregon, for instance, where east of the Cascades, in the Klamath Falls area, you'll find as many as 290 days of sun a year. The southeastern part of the state is also dry with 250 to 300 days of sun and less than 10 inches of rain annually. In central Oregon, there's nothing but blue skies all day long, except for an occasional cloud here and there, which adds up to a miniscule 12 inches of rain a year. In northeastern Oregon, the weather is dry and sunny. The Columbia Gorge is a bit harder to describe since it covers such a broad area, but take my word for the eastern part of it—sunny. Admittedly, weather on the coast can be moody and quite unpredictable. But most people would gladly toss out a few days of sun in exchange for a little excitement in the form of high winds and crashing waves.

Which brings us to beautiful Portland and the Willamette Valley. (Stop here for a moment...and crank open the windows of your mind.) Despite what you may have heard, the Valley has mild temperatures all year round. Summers are sunny; autumns are often clear and dry, and it is merely the winter and early spring that are drizzly and wet. While it rains from November through March, the average annual rainfall in the Valley is still only 40 inches, less than that in many major U.S. destinations, including Chicago and New York. If you want to be precise in your verbal descriptions from now on, remember this: the annual rainfall in the Willamette Valley is less than Miami, Fla., or Nassau in the Bahamas.

Of course, it is winter that sun-worshiping outsiders tend to dwell on. And it's true, our winters are filled with dark and overcast days, but, here again, look at it from the insider's perspective. (That's right. Put yourself in our galoshes.)

In the typical Willamette Valley winter, we have a wealth of wet experiences foreign to people in other climates. There are aural pleasures: the plip-plop of droplets dripping from the eaves, the pitterpatter of rain on a car roof, and the squish-squash of rubber boots on dry linoleum floors. There are visual treasures: the fleeting innocence of tiny yellow rain

Nunan House, Jacksonville / Kenneth Naversen

Historic Ashland / Lynn Radeka

slickers at a school-yard crossing, the moody blues of the barge traffic chugging up the Willamette River, or the soothing pendulum-like swing of windshield wipers on the way home from work. And last, there is that daily, olfactory sensation that beats all the rest: the unmistakably, clean smell of fresh winter rain. The point to all this is that to many western Oregonians, winter rain is sunshine. It's simply in the blood. Come November, I guarantee it, natives vacationing in other states will flock back here in a flash.

And that reminds me of a wibbly, wobbly little tale about how western Oregonians got the nickname webfoots. It all started when...

Aren't They All Lumberjacks?

Now there's one tall tale, and I'm not talking about towering Douglas Firs.

Beautiful Oregon, with its nearly 30 million acres of ever-verdant forests, has long supported the image (to outsiders, at least) of a state full of fallers chopping down trees. Well, it's true, we are the top lumber and plywood producer in the country, which in 1994 accounted for 23 percent of all U.S. lumber production. And it's true, one third of all manufacturing employment in our state is in the forest products industry. But Oregon's economy is about much more than trees. Factors such as the recent recession and mature lumber disappearing quicker than it can be replaced (despite tinkering with growth rates, cloning trees and all that designer gene jazz) have changed the forest industry, and the state has diversified as a result. Looking back, we've probably always had more variety than an outsider might perceive.

Which brings us to the flannel shirt on the lumberjack's back, (which, say the sheepman, has nothing metaphorically to do with straw and camels.) The point here is that woolen mills' have always been a visible part of Oregon's economy, if not for their high sales volume, for the quality of the product. Say "Pendleton" anywhere in the United States, and you'll stir up fond images of grandpa in his red flannel robe, or woolen blankets around side-line spectators. You'll also stir up visions of wool being carded, spun, dyed and woven at the Pendleton Woolen Mills and others throughout the state. Thanks to today's sheep ranchers in central and eastern Oregon, wool production is alive and well. (Incidentally, old movie fans, the eastern part of the state not only has sheep, but cattle, and they're coexisting quite comfortably.)

Throughout Oregon, agriculture is a significant industry, employing 100,000 people. Between 1990 and 1992, the number of Oregon farms increased, while nationally the number of farms decreased. We have productive farm lands in every area of the state: coastal dairylands (the first step in Tillamook cheese), fertile valley soils (responsible for all those berries), Columbia River croplands and orchards, and irrigated desert soils. In total, we produce over 170 different crops and export 80 percent of our products. We are among the top three producing states in peppermint, hops, strawberries, filberts (also known to the marketing wizards by the more appetizing sound of hazelnuts), pears, broccoli and onions. The farmers of the sea are also not to be taken lightly, primarily for the service they offer the salivary glands, in the many prepared forms of Chinook Salmon (our state fish), Dungeness Crab, clams, shrimp and oysters.

Another vital segment of our economy centers on metals and metal fabrication. Here, our strengths have been naturally enhanced by the low-cost hydroelectric power from the mighty Columbia River. While third

Goodpasture Covered Bridge / Dennis Frates

Covered Bridge Interior / Lynn Radeka

world competition and rising energy costs have resulted in closure of most aluminum smelters, our state still employs thousands in the metal and manufacturing industries.

But speaking of industry, the largest industrial employer in Oregon is a high tech firm. You heard it right. The state with all those lumberjacks also has silicon forests. Although the electronics industry in Oregon is not a national leader in any one area, it supplies 32,000 people with jobs. Eighty percent of the high tech firms in the state have their headquarters here, and 75 percent of the total number of these firms have sprung up in the last decade. The downward trend in the electronic industry world-wide has rippled into Oregon.

Because of our strategic location, with the Pacific Ocean providing world-wide access and the Columbia providing inland access, we aren't in the habit of making products and leaving them stranded. Oregon manufacturing is boosted by the 23 ports in our state, with the Port of Portland far and away the leader in import and export trade. Although the port handles only about nine percent of all west coast shipping, it has earned its place as a major port with niches in grain and lumber exports, and automobiles and auto parts imports.

Finally, Oregon's tourism industry is vital to our economy. Third, after agriculture and forest products, tourism plays a starring role throughout the entire state, and is definitely a class act in terms of revenue. (In 1994 alone, tourism brought in over $3 billion.) Our low prices and high-tourist neighbor to the south, California, have helped. But what would tourism be without an abundance of beauty in the form of natural attractions of all degrees in every corner of the state? In beautiful Oregon, we've got them all. And with Paul Bunyan as my witness, that's no tall tale.

But, Is There Culture?

O.K., so we aren't the Big Apple. We don't swoon over Baryshnikov's every move; we don't see a new Broadway show every night; and we don't get regular jolts from MOMA down the street. But, what we do do, right here, is very similar to New York: we get culture at the edge of the wild.

Where else but in Oregon, can you ski down an 11,000 ft. mountain and take in the latest play all in the same day? Sink up to your waist in hip waders at five and up to your elbows in authentic Chinese food at sundown? Travel in body, and spirit, from the heart of the wilderness to the heart of the city in less than an hour? (Or, for that matter, stay in the city the whole darn while, and be thoroughly entertained.)

Oregon's major center of culture is found in Oregon's major city, Portland. There's live entertainment in the form of opera, theatre, ballet, and symphony. We have aesthetically and acoustically fine arenas—the recently renovated Paramount Theatre (now nicknamed the Schnitz), the new Performing Arts Center, and the Civic auditorium. In the summer evenings, many of the city's parks transform into performing arts centers, too, offering patrons a flurry of excitement. You can listen to jazz or blue grass alongside the animals at the zoo, chamber music in the hub of the city at Pioneer Courthouse Square, or big bands echoing through the natural amphitheater in Washington Park. In addition, the city's many private clubs and lounges serve as stimulating springboards for talented jazz and blues musicians, rock groups, and comedians.

Oregon performance arts are not limited to Portland, however. The Hult Performing Arts Center in Eugene, two hours south of Portland, is also known for its exceptional performances. And one of the most noteworthy theatrical groups in Oregon can be found in Ashland, just off of I-5 in

Shakespeare Festival, Ashland / Kenneth Naversen

southern Oregon. Here, each February through October, the Oregon Shakespeare Festival hosts a repertory of both Shakespearean and modern plays presented in two indoor theatres and one outdoor Elizabethan stage. Visitors from all over the world come to savor the experience (and sample the Lithia spring water) in this quaint town nestled in the foothills of the Siskiyou Mountains.

Visual arts are also flourishing in Oregon. The Oregon Art Institute, in Portland, boasts artifacts from ancient China to Native America, as well as paintings from the Renaissance, Impressionist, and here and now. The Institute also satisfies arty appetites with a regular outpouring of classes and lectures. Within walking distance, a smattering of private galleries exhibit their personalities through the works of regional, national and internationally known artists. Art lovers keep the first Thursday of every month open because it's gallery night in Portland.

Other artists and craftsmen are found throughout the state at Saturday markets in Portland and Eugene, as well as nooks and crannies where city, valley, coast, mountains, or desert inspire artistic expression. Those seeking can find glass blowers using a 2000 year-old process, potters dealing with traditional forms, and textile artists designing avant garde fashions.

Whether one credits it to climate, scenery, or sheer native intelligence, Oregon is also the land of fine writers. Oregon natives Ken Kesey (One Flew Over the Cuckoo's Nest), Jean Auel (Clan of the Cave Bear) and science fiction writer Ursula LeGuin are just a few of the many who wield their pens here. In Portland, bibliophiles pilgrimage regularly to Powell's Books, one of the largest bookstores in the world, which covers an entire city block. Here, in the middle of thousands of books covering every subject imaginable (and some unimaginable), poetry readings and theatrical

Columbia River Gorge, Overview Looking East / Craig Tuttle

(Opposite) Multnomah Falls, Columbia River Gorge / Craig Tuttle

performances are free on Monday nights.

And yes, we've got architecture, too. Portland has even been called a microcosm of architectural diversity. Innovative planning and development in recent years has resulted in a towering pink monolith of a bank (Portland's tallest structure), a bold example of Postmodernism via Michael Graves' Portland building, and a striking jail opposite it that looks more like a luxury hotel. From pastel waterfront condominiums to the downtown transit mall, and renovated hotels and office buildings in between, Portland's architecture reflects an Oregon pride.

Other notable architecture is scattered throughout the state, including churches by Portland's Pietro Belluschi, a library by Alvar Aalto, and a house by Frank Lloyd Wright. Colorful Victorian homes in Astoria as well as the historic hill-top Pittock Mansion in Portland speak of a commitment to architectural preservation, which should come as no surprise in our environmentally aware state.

Portland is a great city for film. And that is no illusion. Here, the film buff can slide into her seat in dozens of cinemas, and see old films, current releases, foreign or art films. One of the premier showcases is the Northwest Film and Video Center, a part of the Oregon Art Institute which specializes in international films, both classic and contemporary. While the Portland fan can see every genre from the latest in animation (perhaps by our own Will Vinton) to the latest in adventure, he can also take in the latest in spatial effects of the cinema design around him. Oregon is also a state of international cultures, as illustrated in a Scandinavian festival, an Oktoberfest, and a China Town. The Japanese Gardens in Portland are yet another sterling example of our multi-cultural heritage. Located in Washington Park, these formal gardens are considered one of the most authentic of their kind outside of Japan. Visitors can enjoy the artistic repose of the carefully raked forms in the sand and stone garden, or relish the tranquility in four other traditional gardens and the Ceremonial Tea House. Throughout the gardens, over 50 varieties of Japanese Iris are featured.

Across the street is another garden; the International Rose Test Garden, a visual and aromatic showcase of 8000 bushes and 400 varieties of roses, including every size and color imaginable. The gardens are heavily visited during Portland's 17 day Rose Festival in June, a celebration which includes a grand floral parade and a host of other events, making it the biggest festival of the year in the "Rose City."

And yes, Oregon has a scientific and historical conscience, reflected in over 100 museums throughout the state. In Portland, there is the Oregon Museum of Science and Industry with its interactive exhibitry and continually changing major shows, and the Oregon Historical Society which highlights Oregon and national history. South of Portland, visitors get a peek at culture of days-gone-by in Aurora, the setting of the 19th century Aurora Colonies, the only visible religious commune our state has ever had other than the famous central Oregon "camp" of the now deposed Bhagwhan Shree Rajneesh. In every corner of the state, there's a collection that preserves the flavor of the past or the promise of the future. Get this, New Yorkers: Oregon museums exhibit everything from nautical artifacts to fruit growing memorabilia. And maybe even some big apples.

Columbia River Gorge, West from Hood River / Craig Tuttle

Trillium Lake and Mt. Hood / Craig Tuttle

Now Where Is That Mountain?

A person could move to the Willamette Valley, live here for weeks (even in sunny weather), and never realize that there's a spectacular, snow-covered mountain nearby. Then one day, the cloud cover and fog lounging on the eastern horizon will dissipate, and a powerful, cone-shaped god will appear. This unearthly presence will loom over the surrounding cityscape and countryside like it owns the whole territory. And from everything I know about it, I wouldn't be the one to argue.

The name of the mountain is Mt. Hood, and according to the wisdom of geologists, geographers, and climbers from all over the world, it deserves the respect that its commanding image suggests.

Mt. Hood is Oregon's highest peak, rising up 11,225 feet. It's a link of the Cascade chain, the string of presently dormant volcanoes, any of which could decide at almost any time to blow up like their pouting sibling (whom they still call a saint) in Washington. It's Oregon's most accessible mountain, and perhaps the most majestic, but not the only one worthy of note. We also have Mt. Jefferson, Mt. Bachelor, the Three Sisters and Mt. Mazama, with Crater Lake in its bowl. Mt. Hood, though, seems to be a good one to talk about.

And maybe that's because it's the center of attention of one of the most scenic drives in the state. Known as the Mt. Hood Loop, the route, from Portland, follows U.S. Highway 26 east, joins highway 35 which extends south from Hood River to the east of the mountain, and I-84 along the Columbia River north of the peak.

Travelers on the Loop see the many faces of Hood, in a view that also constantly changes, the closer one gets. Here you can also get varying perspectives on nature in the surrounding green of the Mt. Hood National Forest.

Part of the scenic drive is the Barlow Road, the westward path of pioneer Samuel Barlow and his wagon train. "God never made a mountain but that he provided a place for man to go around it," quipped Barlow, who proved in his round-about journey that Mt. Hood was no exception.

Barlow's trek began in October of 1845, when his seven covered wagons were joined by 23 more. They traveled up what is now Barlow Creek, down the Zig Zag and Sandy Rivers and across the south slope of Mt. Hood. Through snow and rain, the weary travelers wheeled over rugged territory, before reaching Oregon City in December. Later, Barlow petitioned the state legislature for the right to clear the path and build a tollway. He got the go-ahead, construction began in spring, and by August of the next year, the road was ready for travel. Barlow collected the tolls himself for two years. (Just picture Barlow as a tollbooth operator!)

Today, travelers on U.S. 26 can find a replica of the road's tollgate less than a mile above Rhododendron on the mountain's west slope. Some of the tree trunks here still sport deep gashes where ropes were used to slow the wheel-locked wagons' descent.

Travelers continuing on U.S. 26 eventually arrive at Government Camp, near the mountain's base. From there, a much-traveled side trip leads up to Timberline Lodge. Remember the magnificent exterior shots of the hotel in the movie, "The Shining," starring Jack Nicholson? That was Timberline Lodge (and that's as far as the connection goes). The handsome architecture of this rugged structure stands as a tribute to the artists and craftsmen of the Work Progress Administration (W.P.A.), who built it in only 15 months time during the 1930's. The building is now a historical landmark, which gives skiers, hikers and those just-looking, a strong appreciation for the past. While you're at Timberline, you might want to note that Mt. Hood is the only place, other than Oregon's Mt. Bachelor, in the lower 48 states where you can ski all year round. A summer training

Pear Blossoms, Hood River Valley / Craig Tuttle

Spring Flowers and Oak Trees near Hood River / Craig Tuttle

ground for the U.S. ski team is located just above Timberline, a fact that Olympic gold medal skier Bill Johnson, from Sandy, Ore., could easily document. Mt. Hood also supports five of Oregon's 14 developed downhill ski areas. And there are many places just made for hikers, cross-country skiers and snow-shoe enthusiasts, as well.

All you really need to remember of this is that the tallest mountain in Oregon is Mt. Hood, and it deserves a visit. And if you'd like a glimpse from afar, similar to that transient kind of snow-capped treat we have in the Willamette Valley, turn to a photo of the mountain in this book. Good. Now turn the page.

A Desert? In Oregon?

I know about this desolate spot in eastern Oregon (about a day's drive from Portland) which reflects life as it was, a landscape dusted by sagebrush and decorated with sun-cracked hills. I know because a friend told me about it, using words, so protective and powered by emotion, that I've always yearned to visit it. He talked of spending days, searching for arrowheads and never coming up empty handed, of dusks, watching eruptions of color above a monotone terrain, and of nights, endless ones, savoring the solitude.

My friend took his girlfriend there. Then they broke up.

Late the next summer, he drove with anticipation to his special place, pitched his tent on arrival, and soon heard voices. There were two people at the next campsite; one was his former girlfriend.

Needless to say, my friend doesn't buy the notion that no matter how many people you show or tell, some places in that great scheme of things will remain unknown. And from now on, he's not showing—or telling.

And I'd like to tell, but I value my life.

Let's just say there are many comparable places in Oregon's vast desert country, just waiting to coincide with human emotion. It seems that solitude of the desert does for some minds what rhythmic action of ocean waves does for others. The hard terrain does for some hikers what the lush rainforest does for others. And the barren desert landscape provides a striking counter balance to existence in densely populated cities.

Few outsiders think of Oregon as desert country. Instead, they see something closer to a mirage: a totally green and wet state overgrown with trees. Well, one quarter of Oregon is desert. Here, unlike the hot and dry deserts of the Middle East, we have a high desert, which is hot, cold, and dry. It's a wide plateau broken by crevices, and rising into rocky cliffs over 2500 feet high on one edge. Our desert encompasses 28,000 square miles, or as one desert dweller and writer once described it: "Ten good looks across." It includes the counties of Deschutes, Crook, Lake, Harney and Malheur, and overflows into five other states.

Take a good, hard look at the desert, and you'll see the leathery skin of a hardworking cowboy, with a couple days of stubble on his face. The only tree out here is the Juniper, whose gnarled form gives away its age. Sagebrush, rabbit brush, saltbush, and desert grasses support a kind of Puritanical desert attitude. There's no doubt about it, this place speaks of work, not play. Every now and then you do get a treat, in the form of colorful wildflowers—primroses, buttercups, Indian paintbrush, larkspur, phlox, and coral meadow—but they are sparingly dispersed, and perhaps more appreciated because of it.

The Oregon desert is a territory for hunters of Indian artifacts and explorers of homesteader shacks, the rare remnants of our forefathers

First Snow, Mt. Hood National Forest / Craig Tuttle

Proxy Falls, Willamette National Forest / Craig Tuttle

who tried to make a life here and failed. Portions of this barren land are scoured by rockhounders in search of thundereggs (Oregon's state rock), petrified wood, agates, and other semi-precious stones. Those searching can also find hundreds of once active volcanoes.

And speaking of geography, the Oregon desert has the highest exposed geological fault on the continent, as well as one of the world's largest fault blocks. Here, there are remnants of North America's most recent lava flows, and a continuously sprouting geyser. There is a prehistoric, landlocked sea, and a 9,000 acre ponderosa pine forest growing in an area with too little rainfall to make it possible.

And there is much wildlife in this arid place. There are the traditional creatures that come to mind when you think desert: lizards, rattlesnakes, and coyotes. And there also are mule deer, chukar, quail, and pheasant which attract sportsmen during hunting season.

The Oregon desert is home of the largest cattle ranches in the state, as well as acres of irrigated cropland. And sprinkled here are towns, too: places like Prineville, Bend, Redmond, Blitzen, Wagontire, and Brothers. There's even a place by the name of Plush, named by one player in the last round of a feisty poker game who mispronounced flush. (And they called it the wild West!)

The Oregon High Desert Museum, south of Bend, off U.S. 97, is one place that can answer all the questions of the curious. Here, man has entered the picture, in an ambitious effort to provide a living museum which showcases the cultural and natural history of the desert. You'll find indoor and outdoor exhibits of native plants and animals, pioneer and native american historical exhibits, and western art and artifacts. So get a little background, then head back out onto the expansive desert where there is always "plenty of elbow room."

Some people would like to keep it that way.

Ecola State Park / Craig Tuttle

(Opposite) *The Needles at Cannon Beach / Craig Tuttle*

Oregon Dunes near Florence / Craig Tuttle

Newport Bay Bridge and Marina / Craig Tuttle

Pistol Rock Park on South Coast / Craig Tuttle

Boardman State Park / Craig Tuttle

(Opposite) Shore Acres State Park / Craig Tuttle

South Sister from Sparks Lake / Craig Tuttle

Mt. Washington from Big Lake / Zane Holland

(Opposite) Steens Mountain / Craig Tuttle

Smith Rock State Park / Craig Tuttle

The Painted Hills / Craig Tuttle

Mt. Jefferson from Scott Lake / Craig Tuttle

Llama Farm, Sisters / Kenneth Naversen

(Opposite) South Sister from Green Lake / Craig Tuttle

Three Fingered Jack / Craig Tuttle

Mt. Joseph, Wallowa Mountains / Craig Tuttle

I Read About Crater Lake
In My Weekly Reader.

I will never forget that day in third grade. There I was in my little school house in rural Wisconsin, quietly reading, when the frontpage story leapt out at me from the hinged top of my wooden desk. A deep, blue lake, way out in Oregon. A huge water-bowl resting in an extinct volcano. A crater just like they have on the moon! Whew! I don't mind telling you that to an eight year old, in middle America, that's incredible.

To a 32 year old in Portland, it's still incredible.

Crater Lake, cupped at the crest of the Cascades in southern Oregon, is one of those majestic places in the overall scheme of things. No matter how little publicity it gets in a year, it will always be a well-known spot that annually welcomes hoards of tourists from all over the world. It will always be considered amazing and unforgettable. It will never lose its place. It's a natural wonder significant enough in geological history that any person-on-the-street could almost expect to be asked: where were you, what were you doing, and how were you first told about Crater Lake?

Let's take a look at its geological background. Crater Lake rests in a caldera that was formed when a 12,000 foot volcano, Mt. Mazama, collapsed after numerous eruptions. That was nearly 6,600 years ago. Today, the crater's walls rise nearly 2,000 feet in some places from the shores of the nearly 2,000 foot deep lake. (Now imagine the magnitude of that to a child who is just mustering the courage to try the deep-end of the swimming pool.)

Throughout the years, thanks to conservationalists, the pristine waters have remained unspoiled. Aptly called the "crown jewel of the Cascades" by one writer in the 1920's, the precious blue is surrounded by the verdant beauty of the Umpqua, Rogue River and Winema national forests. This entire region of Oregon is sprinkled with scenic and recreational gems such as the nearby Upper Klamath Lake, which is Oregon's largest lake and a haven for a variety of migratory birds, and the Rogue River itself, considered one of the finest fishing streams in the state. None of these attractions quite compares in scope, however, to Crater Lake.

The visitor standing on the crater's rim feels a timeless sense of serenity reflected in the lake. The cone-shaped Wizard Island rises up from the lake's center, the result of an eruption from the caldera floor. Another island, Phantom Ship, resembles a pirate's ship, its jutting rocky forms cutting through virgin waters. Looking out from the eastern shores, Mt. Scott rises majestically in the background.

Winters in this mystical setting find cross-country skiers and snow-shoers traversing on marked trails. Summers, preferably in June or July, find awestruck drivers winding around the 33 mile paved rim drive, still banked with snow. The only way, other than by boat, to explore the lake on its own level is to hike it, and at the same time discover the small treasures within, including colorful meadow wildflowers and abundant pine and fir trees. Overlooking what I view as just about the prettiest lake you'll ever see, is Crater Lake Lodge, a rustic masterpiece which blends into its natural surroundings.

In addition to a powerful, natural history, Crater Lake has an important man-made history, which started with its discovery, accidentally, by a prospector searching for gold in 1852. Although he recorded his find, with ample adjectives describing the depths of the blue lake, no one walked that way again until a decade later, when the powerful impact of the scene was seconded. But it wasn't until the first photographs came out by pioneer photographer Peter Britt, in 1884, that disbelievers were

(Opposite) Wallowa Mountains, Wallowa Lake / Craig Tuttle

John Day Fossil Beds / Craig Tuttle

finally convinced of the spectacular lake. Shortly thereafter, many people began to seek it out.

Over the years, the descriptive titles changed from Deep Blue Lake, Lake Majesty, Sunken Lake, and finally to Crater Lake, which from the geological standpoint is not quite accurate since it really isn't a crater at all, but a caldera. (A crater is the depression forming the outlet of the volcano; a caldera is many times that diameter.) Thanks to our conservationally minded forefathers, the lake and surrounding area became a national park in 1902. It is still Oregon's one and only.

Today, while the natural history of Crater Lake continues on a slow and relatively invisible course, the man-made history is obvious just by picking up a daily newspaper. Recently, a submarine equipped with a video camera was sent to the lake bottom in an effort to find evidence of hot springs activity. Shortly after the research began, geothermal vents were located on the caldera floor, and manned dives into the wild blue yonder are next on the agenda.

Sounds like a scoop for Weekly Reader.

And The Water Is Sooooo Cold...

R umor has it that an offshoot of the polar bear club (sort of a coastal cub-culture) has surfaced in Bandon, Coos Bay, Florence, Newport, Lincoln City, Cannon Beach, Astoria, and every other city up and down Oregon's coast. To be initiated into the club, all one has to do is stick a big toe into Oregon's blue or gray Pacific, anywhere on the 400 mile stretch, at any time, or any season. And that means even in the dead of July. (Note: While the club is not limited to any particular age group or species, it appeals most to human daredevils between the ages of four and 18, and dogs from six months on up.)

Yes, our waters are cold. The Pacific, as we know it in July, ranges in temperature from 52 degrees in the south to 63 degrees up north, not to mention intermittent swells of even cooler water from the depths. This water, however, laps up onto some of the most beautiful beaches in the world.

The Oregon coast has miles of sand-lined beaches and acres of forested capes. It offers diverse recreation from beachcombing to clamming, camping to fishing. And it offers diverse scenery, too: jetting vistas, jagged shores, sheltered coves, and maybe even some sunken treasures.

The best way to experience our coast (alas, the favorite destination of Oregon tourists from in state and out) is to take highway "1-0-1-derful," as one clever writer put it, all the way down.

Starting a few miles off the coast in Astoria, you'll meet the spirit of Oregon past through the colorful Victorian homes sprinkled in the hills, as well as artifacts in The Columbia River Maritime Museum.

Heading south, you'll soon be immersed in the richness of Oregon present. Visitors in Seaside can take a fun-filled stroll on the two mile beachside promenade. Just down the road is the creative community of Cannon Beach, home to many talented artists year round, and the site of a sand castle building contest every summer. Here, too, is the 235 foot high Haystack Rock, a wildlife refuge, and one of the world's most photographed off-shore rocks. Nearby Ecola State Park offers an excellent example of the cleanliness and panoramic beauty of Oregon's coastal parks. (Look for sea lions on the off-shore rocks.)

Continuing south, many majestic cliff-side viewpoints abound, including a route which winds around Neahkahnie Mountain. Local legend has it that treasures were buried by a ship-wrecked Spanish crew on this

Eagle Cap Mountain in Eagle Cap Wilderness / Craig Tuttle

Hell's Canyon and Snake River / Craig Tuttle

mountain centuries ago. (If you've seen Spielberg's "Goonies", perhaps you'll recognize the scenery.)

Farther down the highway, the traveler can cross through the lush dairylands surrounding Tillamook, stop to watch the cheesemaking process, and even steal a taste. Continuing south, and just off of 101, is the scenic Three Capes Loop, where spectacular vistas, a restored lighthouse, and a trail through the rainforest await the curious.

Pacific City is one of many spots along the coast where you can take a day ride on a charter fishing boat after you've taken your Dramamine. Travel out into those bumpy waves and try your luck at landing bottom fish or hooking an unwieldy Salmon, one of Oregon's prime commodities.

Oregon also has its share of motels and condominiums along the coast, especially in the seven mile stretch they call Lincoln City. If you stay here, or almost anywhere on the central or northern coast, take advantage of the wide beaches to relieve any frustrations left over from childhood. (i.e. This is permission to be a kid.) Grab a colorful kite with lots of string and tails, and boost your confidence in these friendly skies, which—yippee—are totally free of trees.

The agenda for the day in Depoe Bay is rise early, climb to a high spot, and watch for gray whales on their yearly 6,000 mile migration south from Arctic waters to Mexico, or on their way back north again. Best viewing times are December through May. To spot one, carefully look for the blow, that spray of condensation up to 12 feet high shooting out of the top of a billowing form, namely a marine mammal up to 45 ft. in length and 45 tons in mass. If you have no luck here, head farther south to Cape Foulweather, and see if you can re-enact the stormy experience of Captain James Cook, who named it.

South is Newport, Oregon's largest coastal city, known for its sport and commercial fishing, and tasty Dungeness Crab. The beaches are a superb place to explore tidal pools. For a little biological background, first visit the Mark O. Hatfield Marine Science Center and Oregon Coast Aquarium, where you'll see, touch, and learn the names of many of the creatures you'll meet. Then, come low tide, position yourself in a rocky outcropping full of waterfilled depressions, and count as many of the green, puff-ball like sea anenomes, purple, spiny sea urchins and symmetrically perfect sea stars (clinging to the rocks for dear life) as you can. The person who counts the most buys dinner at one of the excellent seafood restaurants nearby. If that doesn't suit your tastes, scour the nearby beaches for agates.

Continuing south for miles, the catch word is fish. On Alsea Bay, you'll find crabs, clams, perch and flounder; on the Yachats River, salmon and steelhead.

South of Yachats, where the highway winds around Cape Perpetua, you'll have one last chance at a dramatic view from 800 foot high cliffs before you hit the dunes. Keep your camera out (everyone else will) because just north of Florence is a famous shot you won't want to miss. the Heceta Head Lighthouse. As you continue south, you'll come to the Sea Lion Caves, the only known mainland shelter for the Steller sea lion.

From Florence to Coos Bay, you'll find 40 miles of sand dunes, formed by years of wind and wave slapping against the western foot of the Coast Range. Via dune buggy or camel (rent either one) you'll discover sand piles up to 200 feet in places, and sparkling, fresh-water lakes.

From Coos Bay south to California, some of the least explored, and most exciting beaches on the Oregon coast are waiting. If you climb out on the rocks, be careful not to lose track of time as the surf, in a mesmerizing rhythm, pounds against the jagged forms. Through Coos Bay, you'll pass lumber mills, shipping docks full of ocean-going vessels, and signs indicating that you're in the land of myrtlewood, that golden wood found in many Oregon made products. Head east on Coos River Highway and

Leslie Gulch, Southern Oregon / Craig Tuttle

(Opposite) Walls of Rome, Malheur County / Craig Tuttle

see a grove for yourself.

Farther South, Bandon boasts natural rock sculptures peering down on the beach, a carefully, restored Old Town, and a community pride second to none. For a unique experience, attend a local lecture by the Bandon Storm Watchers.

The spectacular vistas continue from Gold Beach to Brookings. Some of the most striking are encapsulated in the rocky nooks in Boardman State Park, which can also be romantic, depending on your perspective.

This is just a taste of what you can expect to find on the Oregon coast. In the words of one midwest tour director, there are more majestic vistas on Oregon's coast than one would find in the rest of the United States. And if that doesn't shock your senses, dip your toe in our Pacific

We Can Visit. But, Can We Stay?

T he greeting cards are gone now, but they spoke of Oregon's one day of sunshine. And for some reason, the out-of-staters who received them were not even tempted to pull up their sunny stakes, move cross country, and settle with the drips.

And Governor Tom McCall's words urging outsiders "to come, but not stay" didn't help the economic climate very much, either. But both rather unfriendly gestures echoed an attitude that a part of Oregon had harbored for years. Many people here simply felt a personal responsibility to protect this great land.

While Oregon, throughout history, has always had an environmental consciousness—apparent in public ownership of our natural resources at the beginning of the century, the resource projects of the New Deal years, and continued efforts after World War II—there have also been, throughout history, disparaging actions on the part of some, and some of those being outsiders.

One need not look any further than the Willamette Valley to see that. In the 1930's, factories and people dumped everything they could name into the Willamette, a practice which continued into the 60's when the city of Portland became, in the words of one writer, simply a "decaying city dissected by a dirty river." The need for change was apparent .

So the state, under the leadership of McCall, staged a full-fledged clean-up. And it resulted in the transformation of one of most polluted rivers in the world into one of the cleanest.

And today when outsiders dream about Oregon, they might recall the cleansing of the Willamette, or the Scenic Rivers Act. They might remember the bill that forever preserved our beautiful beaches for "free and uninterrupted use" by the public. Or they might think of the bottle deposit bill, or the antiaerosol statute. And perhaps, in a cross country jaunt, they might remember, and not until the service man takes the nozzle out of their hands, that there are no self-service gas stations here. (And maybe that doesn't have much to do with the environment, but the point is this is a special place.)

Throughout the last two decades, Oregon has paid a price in lost business for its environmental commitment. But most Oregonians would feel it has been well worth it, considering the strong base we now have to build on.

Today, Oregon has an outer beauty, apparent in a clean and majestic landscape, and an excellent quality of life.

And today we have an inner glow, too, the result of an improved self-image. Oregonians, in more secure surroundings, have a better attitude toward outsiders. Our state motto? Oregon. You're more than wecome.

Crater Lake / Craig Tuttle

Rear Cover - Willamette National Forest / Craig Tuttle

$12.95

Published by

Beautiful America Publishing Company
T.M.

Wilsonville, OR 97070

ISBN 0-89802-428-5

ISBN 0-89802-428-5

Beautiful America's
Oregon

Gail M. Curtis